World's Cutest CRITTERS

in 3-D

by J. Elizabeth Mills

SCHOLASTIC

New York • Toronto • London • Auckland
Sydney • Mexico City • New Delhi • Hong Kong

World's Cutest Critters in 3-D produced by becker&mayer!
11120 NE 33rd Place, Suite 101
Bellevue, WA 98004
www.beckermayer.com

ISBN 978-0-545-37118-6

10 9 8 7 6 5 4 3 2 1   11 12 13 14 15

Printed in Dongguan, China
First edition, September 2011

becker&mayer!
BOOK PRODUCERS   10482

Written by J. Elizabeth Mills
Edited by Betsy Henry Pringle
Designed by Sarah Baynes
Design assistance by Rosanna Brockley
3-D anaglyph effects by Bill Whitaker and Matthew Fisher
Photo research by Zena Chew
Production management by Jennifer Marx

Photo credits: Front cover: bunny © James Prevette/iStockphoto; koala © Eric Isselée/Dreamstime.com; hedgehog © Lana Langlois/Shutterstock. Title page: chipmunks © Tobias Helbig/iStockphoto. Page 3: wombat © Gerry Pearce/Alamy. Page 4: giraffes © Anna Omelchenko/Shutterstock. Page 5: wolves © Steven Melanson/Dreamstime; bunny and duck © Richard Peterson/Shutterstock. Page 6: slow lorises © John Giustina/Photographer's Choice/Getty Images. Page 7: squirrels © E.P./Shutterstock; orangutan © Eric Isselée/Shutterstock. Page 8: axolotl © Photoshot Holdings Ltd./Alamy. Page 9: pygmy sea horse © David & Debi Henshaw/Alamy; porcupine fish © Steven Hunt/Photographer's Choice/Getty Images. Page 10: koala © Dan Kite/iStockphoto. Page 11: pine martens © Tom Murphy/National Geographic Stock; raccoons © studioworx/Shutterstock. Page 12: owlet © ethylalkohol/Shutterstock. Page 13: tawny owlets © Wim Weenink/Foto Natura/Minden/National Geographic Stock; saw-whet owlet © mlorenz/Shutterstock. Page 14: dormouse © Gerard Lacz/Peter Arnold Images/Photolibrary. Page 15: ermine © Konrad Wothe/Minden Pictures/National Geographic Stock; pygmy marmoset © Mark Finney/flickr/Getty Images. Page 16: grizzly bear family © Yva Momatiuk & John Eastcott/MI/National Geographic Stock. Page 17: giant pandas © Corbis/Photolibrary; polar bear © Peter Kirillov/iStockphoto. Page 18: rabbits © Juniors Bildarchiv/Alamy. Page 19: emperor tamarin baby © Eric Gevaert/Shutterstock; squirrel © shipfactory/iStockphoto. Page 20: flamingo © Edwin Verin/Dreamstime. Page 21: red-eyed tree frog © Snowleopard1/iStockphoto; peacock © Rainlady/iStockphoto. Page 22: dog and cat © fury123/iStockphoto. Page 23: pandas © Dani Vincek/Shutterstock; squirrel monkeys © Eric Gevaert/Shutterstock. Page 24: baby goat © rtyree1/iStockphoto. Page 25: chick © Volina/Shutterstock; piglet © Michaela Stejskalova/Shutterstock. Page 26: cat and dog © GK Hart/Vikki Hart/Stone/Getty Images. Page 27: sea otters © Tom Soucek/Alaska Stock LLC/Alamy; sea turtle cleaning station © Masa Ushioda/SeaPics.com. Page 28: dolphin © Skynesher/iStockphoto. Page 29: gentoo penguin © javarman/Shutterstock; pandas © rehoboth foto/Shutterstock. Page 30: chameleon © Ian Nichols/National Geographic Stock. Page 31: loris © Dani & Jeske/Photolibrary; baby monkey © benkei1975/Shutterstock. Page 32: stoat © Ronnie Howard/Shutterstock. Page 33: polar bear © Paul Nicklen/National Geographic Stock; Weddell seal © Serget/Dreamstime. Page 34: arctic fox © Richard Codington/Alamy. Page 35: jackals © p.schwarz/Shutterstock; pika © Kenneth Rush/Shutterstock. Page 36: fawn © Jerry Mayo/iStockphoto. Page 37: koala © Matthew Jones Photography/iStockphoto; red panda © Stef Bennett/Dreamstime. Page 38: fennec foxes © dean bertoncelj/Shutterstock. Page 39: fawn © johnsfon/iStockphoto; rabbit © Paul Murphy/Dreamstime. Page 40: elephants © Malsbury Enterprises Ltd/iStockphoto. Page 41: lions © Moodville/Dreamstime; orangutans © Freder/iStockphoto. Page 42: red fox pups © Jim Kruger/iStockphoto. Page 43: polar bears © Dave Parsons/iStockphoto; giant pandas © ChinaFotoPress/Getty Images News. Page 44: cheetahs © Purdy Photography/iStockphoto. Page 45: boxfish © Stubblefield Photography/Shutterstock; zebras © Suelane/Dreamstime. Page 46: foals © Maria Itina/Dreamstime. Page 47: elephants © Johan W. Elzenga/iStockphoto; tigers © hxdbzxy/Shutterstock. Page 48: bear cub © Mihai Dancaescu/Shutterstock. Back cover: hedgehog © Eric Isselée/Shutterstock; chick © Ljupco Smokovski/Dreamstime.com; mouse © Eric Isselée/Shutterstock; red panda © Eric Isselée/Dreamstime.com; guinea pig © Sascha Burkard/Dreamstime.com.

Awesome Animals

Hello! Are you ready to play?

Welcome to the wild, wonderful, furry, and fuzzy animal kingdom. In this book, you'll meet cute critters that climb, sleep, play, and dance, just like you do! Some animals are itty-bitty, and some are huge. Some have fur, and some have fins. The 3-D glasses included with this book will make you think all these animals are so close that you can touch them!

So punch out and assemble your 3-D glasses, turn the page, and get ready to go nose-to-nose with the world's cutest critters!

Best Friends

Our spots match perfectly!

You look that way, and I'll . . .

At up to 19 feet tall, giraffes are the tallest animals on land. These long-necked and long-legged animals can see over trees to watch for danger. Giraffe friends take turns drinking at water holes so that one of them is always on the lookout.

What did you say?

Have you ever heard a dog howl? Wolves howl, too. Wolves and dogs are related, and both use body positions and howls to let their packs know how they're feeling. Sometimes a pack of wolves howls together in a nighttime chorus.

Can I rest my head on yours?

Pint-size pals

It's nice to have a friend who's the same size as you, and just as fuzzy. Baby bunnies are born without any fur, but after about ten days they have a coat of soft fuzz. When ducklings hatch, they are covered in downy fuzz.

Quack! Ready to play hopscotch?

Just Hangin' Out

Takin' it slow and easy . . .

Climb time

Have you ever tried hanging by your feet? Tree-dwelling slow lorises do it all the time! Hanging by their toes keeps their hands free to hold on to other branches or food. Special blood vessels in their feet and hands allow slow lorises to "hang out" for hours at a time. Do you wish you could hang out with them?

Upside-down snack

Squirrels love to do two things—climb and eat! They scamper up and down tree trunks and leap from branch to branch. Squirrels can even eat while hanging upside down. There are about 270 kinds of squirrels around the world. Some are as tiny as your hand, and some are as big as your arm!

Come hang with us!

High and dry

Orangutans live in trees. They use their arms to swing from branch to branch. These clever apes use everyday objects like leaves and twigs as tools. They make leaf umbrellas to keep themselves dry in the rain. Keeping dry comes in handy when you live in a rain forest!

I love my tree trapeze!

Our Finny Friends

Pink is my favorite color!

Silly salamander

Funny-looking axolotls have a lot in common with fish. They live in water, and they breathe through gills. But they have skin instead of scales, and they have legs, so they are not fish. Axolotls are salamanders with a special ability—they can grow another leg if they lose one!

Undersea pygmy

Pygmy sea horses rarely grow bigger than 1 inch. To stay hidden from fish that might want to eat them, their bodies mimic, or match, the color and shape of the coral where they live. They hide so well that scientists aren't sure how many pygmy sea horses live in the ocean!

What color should I be today?

Spike!

Porcupine fish move slowly and look clumsy in the water. But they have a secret way of defending themselves against bigger fish—they inhale water and blow themselves up into big, spiky balls.

Aw, I'm just a giant softy.

Tree Huggers

**Want to come sit with me?
There's room for two!**

The best seat

Koalas have thick gray or brown fur that keeps them warm, protects them from rain, and gives them a cushion for a nap in the eucalyptus trees. Koalas rely on the trees for food and shelter. These tree-dwelling marsupials live only in Australia, and that country has passed laws to keep them safe.

Sky-high pals

Look up! You might see a pair of pine martens leaping from one branch to the next. Often found in Alaska, Canada, the Pacific Northwest, the Rocky Mountains, and northern New England, pine martens use their sharp claws to scamper through the trees.

Catch us if you can!

Afternoon paws

Could you climb down from a tree headfirst? Raccoons can! They use their claws to hold on to the tree trunk. A raccoon's paws look a lot like your hands. They use their paws to grab objects, hold them, and pull them apart, just like you do.

Are we having fun yet?

Whoo's So Cute?

Watch me! I'm an expert flier!

Flight school

Young owls are often born in tree hollows like this one. Soon they develop muscles and feathers that help them fly. A grown-up owl will wait on a high perch and then swoop down to grab a meal. Owls fly so quietly that their prey doesn't hear them coming.

All fluffed up

Birds shake out their feathers for many reasons: to preen and groom them, to air them out after cleaning, to offer a cheerful greeting, or to add a layer of air in cold weather to help keep warm. It's like putting on a down jacket!

It's good to be warm together!

Want to play "I Spy"?

Big eyes

Owls have eyes that face forward and act like binoculars, just like your eyes do. But owls also have flexible necks, so they can see what is behind them. Some can swivel their heads three-quarters of the way around.

Hide-and-Seek

Squeak! I see you!

Ready or not . . .

Most dormice are nocturnal, which means they come out to play at night and sleep during the day. They can tuck into tiny tree hollows, which are perfect for hide-and-seek! When it's time to play, they chatter with other dormice using a variety of sounds.

Here I . . .

An ermine has two coats—a brown one for summer, and a white one for winter. But the tip of its tail is black all year long. These sleek animals are low to the ground. An ermine has short legs and a long body that slides in and out of holes easily.

Oops, I forgot to wear my summer coat!

Come!

Pygmy marmosets are tiny and blend in with their surroundings. This makes them hard to see. These quick-moving monkeys love playing high up in the treetops of South American rain forests.

You found me!

Beary Adorable

And for my next trick—walking on my hind legs!

Talent contest

During the winter months, mama grizzlies go into their dens to give birth to their cubs. These hardworking moms care for their cubs for two to three years. Mother bears teach their young how to hunt, fish, and defend themselves. But cubs don't need lessons on how to be beary adorable!

Just chillin'

Shy pandas are not shy about eating! They chomp on as much as 85 pounds of bamboo each day. Half of every day is spent eating. Giant pandas live in dense forests at elevations of 4,000 to 13,000 feet, hidden away in the misty mountains of China.

You won't get lost—I'll hold your hand.

Champion swimmer

Large, webbed paws help polar bears glide through the cold Arctic waters. These furry giants use their front paws to move and their back legs to steer. Polar bear paws have rough pads to help them walk on slippery ice.

Oh, I love posing for pictures!

"Just a Nibble

This leaf is just right for both of us.

Yum!

Do you like salad? Rabbits do. Rabbits have special teeth that help them chew high-fiber leaves, grass, and other plants. Their teeth are constantly growing, so bunnies gnaw and nibble to keep their teeth from getting too long. Rabbits live in meadows, woods, and grasslands, where there is always plenty to nibble on.

Clean teeth

Tamarins snack on plants, and they also love to eat fruit during the rainy season and sweet nectar and sap during the dry season. Central and South American forests provide lots of yummy food options for these adorable monkeys.

Yum! Tree sap is my favorite treat.

Go nuts!

Squirrels are clever. Before winter comes, they gather and store food so they will have plenty to eat when the weather turns cold. Squirrels eat nuts, seeds, plants, and insects. Like bunnies, squirrels have teeth that never stop growing. They gnaw constantly to keep their teeth healthy.

Munch, crunch—nuts for lunch!

Colorful Critters

I can stand on one leg . . . can you?

Pretty in pink

With bright pink feathers and long, skinny legs, flamingos are easy to spot. Their diet of small shrimp makes them pink. Flamingos use their long legs to wade into deep water and find food. Their big bills suck in water and filter out the shrimp.

Hop to it

A red-eyed tree frog may look only green at first. But when it senses danger, it will open its bright red eyes and show its bright blue legs with orange feet. The vivid colors surprise and confuse the enemy. Then the tree frog can hop away safe and sound.

It's not easy being bright and colorful!

Strut your stuff

Male peacocks are the fanciest birds in the animal kingdom. When a peacock fans out its train, shiny blue and green feathers catch the sunlight. This display dazzles female peacocks, called peahens.

Do you like my do?

Snuggle Buddies

Is it time for our next nap?

Cuddle time

Who knew dogs liked catnaps? Cats and dogs can be good friends, especially if they meet when they are little. Cats tend to be active at night, so they like to nap during the day. And dogs are always ready for a little snooze.

So soft

A panda's thick coat keeps it toasty warm. Scientists think the black and white colors help pandas blend in with snow and rocky surroundings. This camouflage helps keep them safe. When they're not eating bamboo, pandas nap.

Now we're twice as cozy!

Piggyback

Squirrel monkeys dwell in rain forests in Central and South America. These active animals live in large groups of up to 500 monkeys. A piggyback nap lets a baby get some rest, away from all that monkey business!

I'll just snooze on the go. . . .

Fun on the Farm

Just kidding around

Goats are useful animals on a farm. Their milk can be made into cheese and butter. Their wool is spun into fiber. Baby goats are called kids. When a baby goat gets older, it will grow horns and a beard!

I . . . smell . . . a friend who wants to romp with me!

Peep!

Not all chicks are yellow. Some are a mottled brown and white and some are solid black. No matter what color they are, these farmyard fuzz balls are "peep-le" pleasers!

Who's the coolest chick on the farm?

Pigging out

Pigs are smart, social animals that love to graze, snort, and roll around in the mud. Pigs can learn tricks and are sometimes kept as pets. In France, pigs use their keen sense of smell to find fancy wild fungi called truffles.

Old MacDonald had a pig . . . oink, oink, oink!

Bath Time

You missed a spot . . . right . . . there!

What are friends for?

Cats take cleaning themselves very seriously. They use their rough tongues to groom and smooth their fur. These flexible felines can stick one leg up in the air for extra reach. Sometimes, a friendly dog's big tongue can help out, too!

Surf's up!

Sea otters spend most of their time in the ocean. But the cold water doesn't bother them! Otters have thick fur that keeps them warm and afloat. When bathing, an otter can stretch out and groom any part of its body. These critters are flexible!

We oughter float . . . we're otters!

Fish wash

Even sea turtles need a bath! Turtle shells become covered in algae, tiny plants that live in water. The turtles visit areas in the ocean called cleaning stations. There, special fish nibble away the algae and clean off the shell. It's a perfect partnership!

Thanks, friends. Now I'm all clean!

Let's Boogie

Shall we dance?

DJ

What's a dance party without music? Dolphins are social animals. They moan, squeak, groan, whistle, and grunt. Dolphins send messages about danger, food, and staying together. These vocal marine mammals also make sounds that are too high pitched for humans to hear.

Flippin' out

Penguins look a little silly on the ice—waddling about or sliding on their tummies. But underwater, penguins zoom, flip, dive, and dart in a chilly water ballet! A penguin's coloring gives it a built-in fashionable wardrobe for every dance.

I can do the two-step!

Would you scratch our bellies?

Roly-poly

Young pandas learn important life skills through play. Can you do a panda somersault?

Handy Hands

What a pretty flower . . . I must touch it!

Stre-e-etch!

Chameleons use their long tongues to grab things. They also have special feet with joined toes and claws to help them grip bark. A long tail wraps around branches to help them climb. Colorful chameleons usually live in trees and bushes, but some live on the ground.

Funky fingers

A tree-dwelling loris has unusual hands and feet. Its second finger is much smaller than the others, and its big toe is set far apart from the other toes—like a thumb. This helps it grasp and hold on to branches.

Gimme five!

Cool tools

Rhesus monkeys are good climbers and swimmers, but they spend most of their time on the ground. They use their nimble hands for grooming, playing, and digging. These social monkeys enjoy one another's company. They live in groups called troops. Rhesus troops can have up to 200 members!

You don't mind if I dig some holes here, do you?

Snow Day

Hmmm . . . do I smell lunch?

Good scents

Stoats, a type of weasel, use their sharp sense of smell to track down food. When a stoat tracks prey, it stays close to the ground and runs back and forth in a zigzag. White winter coats keep stoats hidden until they strike!

Snow bear

Though polar bears mostly hunt in the sea, they also hunt on land. Their thick fur keeps them warm in the Arctic weather. Even the bottoms of their feet have fur!

Look! I made a snowball!

Sealed with a kiss

Weddell seals can sometimes be found in large packs out on the ice. Most of the time, though, they stay underwater, to hunt for food and to avoid predators. Weddell seals can stay underwater for 45 minutes; then they swim to a hole in the ice to catch a breath.

Can you do the flipper wave with me?

33

You Can't See Me, Can You?

Winter is my favorite time of year!

Wintry ghost

Arctic foxes have warm fur that changes color with the seasons. In winter, their white coats blend in with the snow and ice. This keeps them hidden from predators and enables them to hunt unseen. Sometimes arctic foxes follow polar bears to find food.

Hiding in plain sight

Jackals live in deserts, savannas, and grasslands, where there aren't many good hiding places. But they usually come out at dawn and dusk, so the low light helps them blend in with the grass and dirt. Jackals can hide in plain sight!

If we stay perfectly still, can you still find us?

Rocky road

Mountain pikas are found in mountainous areas in the western United States and southwestern Canada. They burrow in rock crevices and do not hibernate during the winter. Fur on the soles of their feet helps keep pikas warm as they run over the ice-cold rocks.

Do I look like a furry rock?

Fuzzy Snoozin'

I like my soft, grassy bed!

Stayin' cool

To escape the summer heat, deer slip into cool forests for naps. The spots on a fawn's back help keep it hidden in the shade. Deer usually stay in the forests, away from predators, until dawn or dusk.

Treetop sleep

How much do you sleep each day? Koalas snooze for as many as 18 hours a day in gently swaying eucalyptus trees. They're sleep experts! Koalas are nocturnal, which means they are more active at night. Rather than traveling in a big group, these shy animals tend to keep to themselves.

If you don't mind, I think I'll just . . . zzz!

Fuzzy blanket

Red pandas live in cool mountainous areas in Nepal, Burma, India, and China. They wrap their bushy tails around themselves to stay warm as they sleep high up in the branches.

I'm all snuggled in my tree!

Ear I Am!

We have cool ears, don't you think?

Wings or ears?

Fennec foxes are the smallest foxes. But their ears more than make up for their small size! Those big ears aren't just for show. Fennec foxes live in hot deserts, and blood vessels in their long ears release body heat. This helps the foxes stay cool.

My, what big ears I have!

Ears all around

Mule deer have excellent hearing. This helps them stay safe. A deer can rotate its large ears to listen in all directions. If a white-tailed deer hears danger, it can run away at speeds reaching up to 30 miles an hour.

Sniff, sniff, hop, hop— let's play chase!

What's that sound?

Like deer, rabbits can rotate their ears to listen for sounds all around them. And like a fennec fox's ears, a rabbit's silky-soft ears transfer body heat to the surrounding air. Let's hear it for ears!

Mom and Me

Thanks, Mom. You're the best!

Have trunk, will travel

You might think a long nose would get in the way. But an elephant uses its trunk for all kinds of things: finding food, snorkeling, drinking, eating, trumpeting, and hugging baby elephants. Such a handy body part!

Just lion around

Lions live in groups called prides. The lionesses hunt at night and care for all the cubs in the pride, not just their own. Male lions keep the pride safe with loud roars.

Stay close, little one. I'll look after you.

Smooch

Orangutan mothers care for their young for at least six years. Mothers teach youngsters how to swing from tree branches, build nests, and find food. The mothers want to be sure their young know everything they need to know before they go off on their own.

I love you, Mom!

Recess!

Do you see what we see?

Foxy fun

Foxes live in forests, grasslands, mountains, and deserts. You can also find them living near people. They are intelligent and skillful hunters. Young foxes, called kits, learn and practice important skills as they play with their parents and with other kits.

Polar play

Polar bears have thick layers of fat, called blubber. Blubber helps keep them warm in the Arctic ice and freezing water.

Let's play patty-cake!

Three's company

Panda recess means games of chase and tree climbing. Pandas are usually solitary animals, but they will sometimes play with one another and leave scent messages for other pandas.

Who's king of the tree?

What's the Pattern?

You spotted us!

Speed spots

How fast can you run? Cheetahs are the fastest land animals. These spotted cats can race at up to 70 miles an hour for short periods of time. That's about the speed of a car on the highway.

Pretty b...

Yellow boxfish are foun... in coral reefs. These fish squirt water out of their mouths to stir up dirt in the water. This helps them find algae and other tiny animals that are hiding. Square yellow bodies and bright markings make yellow boxfish easy to "spot" in the ocean.

that my eye, or another spot? Are you sure?

Black and white

No two zebras have the exact same stripe pattern. A herd of zebras looks like a black-and-white wall, especially when the zebras are running. This makes it hard for predators to pick out an individual animal.

We think our stripes look amazing!

Summer Lovin'

Will you be my friend?

Color-foal

A young horse is called a foal until it is one year old. Then it is called a yearling. Foals can stand and run soon after they're born. Horses come in all kinds of colors: black, brown, white, chestnut, and even spotted. Bays are reddish brown, with black manes and tails. A palomino horse has a golden coat and a white mane and tail.

Leggo my nose, silly!

Tug-of-war

Elephant families are close-knit, and members stay together. The oldest mother is in charge of the herd, finding food and water holes. Elephants take care of their young and play together. They use their trunks to touch and caress one another.

Water play

With their stripes and long teeth, tigers are easy to recognize. They are the biggest wildcats. But unlike their cousins, house cats, tigers are good swimmers and seem to enjoy water. They will go into pools to stay cool in the hot summer.

Let's make a splash!

When I'm happy, I like to dance!

I can bearly hold still!

The animal kingdom is full of smart and adorable animals of all kinds. It's our responsibility to respect them, care for them, and look after the environment so these animals can continue to live for a long, long time.

With so many lions, monkeys, bunnies, bears, and more, to choose from, which critter would you say is the cutest?